Some pets are **big**.

My dog is grand.

John F.
Kennedy

John F. Kennedy

I. MacSiccar

JG PRESS

Published in the USA 1995 by JG Press
Distributed by World Publications, Inc.

The JG Press imprint is a trademark of
JG Press, Inc.
455 Somerset Avenue
North Dighton, MA 02764

Produced by
Brompton Books Corporation
15 Sherwood Place
Greenwich, Connecticut 06830

ISBN 1-57215-029-7

Printed in China

Page 1: Aboard the *Honey Fitz* in the summer of 1963.

Pages 2-3: Kennedy gives the commencement address at
American University in Washington, D.C., in June 1963.

Pages 4-5: Family portrait: John, Sr. and Jackie with Caroline and
John, Jr., 1962.

CONTENTS

"IF YOU CAN'T BE CAPTAIN, DON'T PLAY"

When, in October 1914, petite and pretty 24-year-old Rose Fitzgerald married young Joseph P. Kennedy, a good many of her friends probably thought she might have done better. Rose was, after all, the daughter of the celebrated John ("Honey Fitz") Fitzgerald, Boston's first native-born Irish-American mayor, then completing his seventh flamboyant term in office. And since Rose had often acted as her father's official hostess, she had long been acquainted with some of the most important men in local, state, and national political life.

But young Joe Kennedy was not (then) of that ilk. Though his father had been prominent in Massachusetts politics, whatever interest Joe might have had in public affairs seemed always to have been subordinate to his intensely competitive, almost obsessive passion for making money. To be sure, in that respect he was already fairly impressive. Only five years out of Harvard, he had just been elected president of the Columbia Trust Company, thus becoming the youngest bank president in Massachusetts, and, probably, in the country. It was therefore not impossible to imagine that he might someday become – as he himself confidently predicted – a rich man. But it would have taken an uncannily prescient wedding guest to foresee that he and Rose would also be the founders of one of twentieth-century America's greatest political dynasties and the parents of one of the nation's most memorable and charismatic presidents.

That future president, John Fitzgerald Kennedy, was born on May 29, 1917, at a time when his parents were

Previous pages. Jack Kennedy (r.) and his brother Joe at Hyannis Port *c.*1925.

Above: Jack's father, Joseph P. Kennedy, as he looked in 1912, two years before his marriage to Rose Fitzgerald.

Left: Jack's grandfather on his mother's side was John ("Honey Fitz") Fitzgerald, Boston's first native-born Irish-American mayor. He is shown here (center) in 1907.

Right: Jack's mother, Rose Fitzgerald, as she looked in 1911, three years before her marriage to young Joseph P. Kennedy in 1914.

Left: Joe Kennedy with his two sons in 1919. Joe, Jr., is on the left and two-year-old Jack on the right.

Right top: The Kennedys in 1931. From the left: Bobby, Jack, Kathleen, Jean, Joe, Sr., Rose (behind), Patricia, Rosemary, Joe, Jr., Eunice.

Right bottom: The celebrated "Compound," the summer home of the Kennedys at Hyannis Port on Cape Cod, Massachusetts.

still living in their first, rather modest house in the Boston suburb of Brookline. John was, in fact, their second child, his elder brother, Joseph, Jr., having been born two years earlier. Then Rosemary was born in 1918 and Kathleen in 1920, whereupon the family moved in a larger Brookline house where three more children were born: Eunice in 1921, Patricia in 1924, and Robert in 1925.

During this first decade of Rose and Joe's marriage Joe's material fortunes soared. He had made an enviable reputation as a tough, can-do executive working for the Bethlehem Shipbuilding Corporation in World War I, and at the same time he had embarked on what would prove to be a spectacularly successful career as a Wall Street speculator. By 1926 he would also begin to move into the lucrative movie industry, becoming president and chairman of Film Booking Offices of America. Although it is difficult to say precisely when he made his first million, it was probably before John's fifth birthday.

In 1926 the family moved to New York, first to the fashionable Riverdale section of the Bronx and then, in 1929, to an 11-bedroom red-brick mansion in Bronxville in southern Westchester County. By this time the Kennedy's had also acquired an alternative winter home in Palm Beach, Florida, and a big white summer house – the famous "compound" – at Hyannis Port on Cape Cod. And still the clan continued to grow: Jean was born in 1928, and the last child, Edward, in 1932 (by which time John was nearly 15 and already away from home in prep school).

That the Kennedy children grew up surrounded by wealth, privilege, and parental love was undoubted, but their early years were not, on that account, necessarily very relaxed. This was in part due simply to the fact they belonged to a big, boisterous family, but it was probably due even more to the influence of their father's dominating personality. Joe, Sr., was an extremely tough and competitive man, and he wanted his

Left: Edward Kennedy (left) and Jack man a halyard on a family boat at Hyannis Port.

Left below: Edward snares a pass from Jack on the lawn before the "Compound".

Right: Jack, as he looked when he was an undergraduate at Harvard in the late 1930s.

Right below: Harvard's 1937 Junior Varsity Football team. Jack is in the third row, second from the right.

children – especially the boys – to be the same. For him, winning and excelling were everything; second best would never do. "If you can't be captain," he told his sons, "don't play." He actively encouraged competitive rivalries among his children, while at the same time insisting that they always be loyal to, and protective of, one another. It was not an impossible prescription, but it must have been an uncommonly difficult, and probably stressful, one for young children to try to follow.

Not surprisingly, competitive sports such as softball and touch football were the order of the day during the summers at Hyannis Port, as were swimming, sailing, hiking, and all manner of family games. Even bicycling could turn into an all-out contest: in one such race Joe, Jr., and Jack contrived to crash head-on into one another at full speed, with Jack subsequently needing some 20 stitches taken. Jack was, in fact, never a natural athlete like his older brother, but, true to the Kennedy code, that only made him try harder.

When Jack was 13 he was sent to the Canterbury School, a Catholic boarding school in New Milford, Connecticut, but during the spring term he had to have an emergency appendectomy and was unable to complete the school year. The following autumn (1931) he was sent to the same college preparatory school into which Joe, Jr., had entered two years earlier: the Choate School in Wallingford, Connecticut.

By the time Jack came to Choate, Joe, Jr., was already one of the student body's outstanding athletes and scholars, but Jack was destined to be neither. His grades were low, he was too slight to make the varsity football squad, he was plagued by a succession of illnesses, and his rebellious manner caused some raised

eyebrows among the masters. When he was graduated in 1935 he ranked only 64th in a class of 112.

That summer, Joe, Sr., sent Jack – as he had earlier sent Joe, Jr. – to England for a brief course of study at the London School of Economics. But again illness (apparently hepatitis) intervened, and Jack was forced to return home almost as soon as the course began. For the remainder of the summer he flirted with the idea of enrolling in Princeton, but in the end he again bowed to family tradition and that fall entered Harvard, where Joe, Jr., was by now an honor student, on the varsity football squad, and an officer of his class.

For Jack, it seemed at first that Harvard might be a repetition of Choate. During his first two years his grades were generally mediocre, and in his sophomore year he again failed to make the varsity football squad because of his low weight. Worse, during a junior varsity scrimmage that year he sustained a severe back injury – a ruptured lower lumbar disc – that not only ended all possibility of his playing football at Harvard but would cause him considerable pain for the rest of his life.

But things began to look up for him during his junior year. His father, Joe, Sr., had long since moved up from mere wealth to being one of the richest men in America, and his lavish contributions to the Democratic party throughout the 1930s had made the Roosevelt administration increasingly beholden to him. In 1938 Franklin

Left: Jack in 1940, the year he was graduated from Harvard.

Right: A formal portrait of the Kennedy clan *c.*1938.

Right bottom: Jack in Egypt in 1939.

Roosevelt had repaid the debt by appointing Joe, Sr., ambassador to Britain's Court of St. James, and soon thereafter Jack got Harvard's permission to spend the spring semester of this junior year (1939) working for his father overseas. For the next seven months he toured Europe and the Near East, writing badly spelled reports on a world about to plunge into global war.

How useful these reports were to the embassy in London is debatable, but the exercise was certainly good for Jack. Among other things, it provided him with the topic of his senior thesis: *Appeasement at Munich: The Inevitable Result of the Slowness of the British Democracy to a Change from a Disarmament Policy.* It's con-

voluted subtitle notwithstanding, the thesis found favor with Jack's mentors in the Harvard political science department, and he was graduated *cum laude* in 1940. Subsequently, Arthur Krock, a journalist friend of Joe, Sr., undertook to have Jack's thesis published. Much edited, and retitled *Why England Slept*, it sold 80,000 copies.

This was heady wine, indeed, for a 23-year-old who had previously been considered not much more than a rich, albeit plucky, underachiever. Now, perhaps for the first time in his life, Jack Kennedy could think that he might at last be moving out from under the long shadow cast by his accomplished elder brother.

PT 109

Being graduated with honors from college is one thing; deciding what to do next is another. In his Harvard yearbook Jack had listed the law as his intended vocation, but that may have been somewhat *pro forma*. Joe, Jr., was already in his second year in the Harvard Law School and was, as usual, doing splendidly, and Jack might well have felt disinclined to follow again in his formidable brother's footsteps. In any case, he never did apply to a law school but instead enrolled that September (1940) in Stanford University, with the vague intention of auditing some courses in business administration and political science. Whatever problems he was having in making up his mind about his future would, however, soon be made irrelevant by world events.

Europe had been at war for a year, and the United States, despite the clamorous efforts of pacifists and isolationists, was inexorably drifting closer to involvement in the conflict. Joe, Sr., in a series of remarkably unambassadorial public speeches (that greatly annoyed Roosevelt) had denounced the idea that America might ever join Britain in the war against Hitler, but at least he – and Jack – supported American military preparedness, so neither father nor son had reason to complain when, in October 1940, Jack's name was among the first drawn in the new national draft lottery.

Jack was not called up until the following July, at which time he applied for a commission in the U.S. Navy: he became Ensign Kennedy in September. Initially assigned to an intelligence unit in Washington, D.C., he had the bad fortune to begin dating a Danish woman journalist who, it subsequently turned out, was then under FBI surveillance as a possible Axis spy. Even

Previous pages: Jack with the original crew of PT 109. At 10 crewmen, the boat was at first under-complement.

Above: The photo of Jack in his Harvard yearbook.

Left: Ensign John Kennedy at the sixth Naval District headquarters in Charleston, S.C., in 1942.

Right: Jack poses with Rose and Eunice before Sugar Loaf Mountain in Rio de Janeiro in 1941, a few months before he entered the U.S. Navy.

Left: Elco 80-foot PT boats at speed. PT 109 was a unit of this famous class.

Far left below: Joe, Sr., and Joe, Jr., now (May 1942) an ensign and a pilot in the U.S. Navy air corps.

Left below: Lieutenant (JG) John F. Kennedy on Tulagi in May 1942, while PT 109 was still working up to combat-ready status.

Right: Jack on the spartan bridge of PT 109.

more unfortunately, she mentioned Jack by name in a newspaper article that was published just 10 days before the Japanese attack on Pearl Harbor. The embarrassed Navy whisked Jack out of Washington and out of intelligence and gave him an innocuous desk job in Charleston, South Carolina.

But now that America was in the war (and perhaps also, now that Joe, Jr., was training to be a Navy combat pilot), no desk job could possibly satisfy Jack. He badgered the Navy for a transfer, underwent extensive therapy to improve his injured back, and finally, in October 1942, was rewarded by being sent to the Motor Torpedo Boat Training Center at Melville, Rhode Island. After graduation, which qualified him to command a PT boat, he was chagrined to find himself assigned to a series of stateside units, but he got his father to intervene with the secretary of the Navy, and finally, in March 1943, he was posted to combat duty in the South Pacific.

His destination was Tulagi, in the war-torn Solomons, and when his final transport, an LST, neared the island it was subjected to such violent Japanese air attack that nearly a week passed before the craft could safely put Jack on shore. Once on Tulagi, Jack was assigned a somewhat war-weary 80-foot plywood Elco, armed with 50-cal and 20mm automatic weapons and four 21-inch torpedoes and designated PT 109. It took him about a month to repair and refurbish the boat and

to train his new crew, but by the end of May, when now-Lieutenant (JG) Kennedy had just turned 26, PT 109 was deemed combat-ready. By mid-July she, along with about 25 other boats, was sent up to the advanced PT base on Lumbari Island, between the larger islands of Rendova and New Georgia.

The focus of action in the Solomons area at this point in the war was the hotly-contested American effort to capture Japanese-held New Georgia and Kolombangara islands. The Japanese were supplying and reinforcing their garrisons on the islands via heavily-escorted "Tokyo Express" convoys that ran in almost nightly, and among the U.S. Navy units detailed to try to intercept these convoys were the PT boats.

PT 109 was soon involved in a number of fierce, confused night actions, but though some of her crew suffered injuries, the boat remained relatively unscathed throughout the remainder of July. Then, on the night of August 1-2, PT 109 (now with a 37mm cannon added to her armament) and 14 other boats attacked a destroyer-escorted "Express" coming up the Blackett Strait south of Kolombangara. None of the PT flotilla's torpedoes struck home, but the Japanese formation was broken up, and in the ensuing confusion IJN destroyer *Amagiri* suddenly loomed out of the darkness, rammed PT 109, and cut her in half.

Two of the boat's 13-man crew were killed in the collision, and several others were badly injured, but the sur-

vivors were able to cling to the floating wreckage until they spotted a small island three miles distant and were able to swim over to it, Jack the while towing a wounded machinist's mate. When all were safely on shore Jack went back into the sea and spent most of the night swimming about in the vain hope of locating a patrolling PT boat. No rescuers materialized the following day or the day after, and on August 4th the exhausted castaways were obliged to make another three-hour swim to a neighboring island in search of food. What they found was inadequate, so Jack and another officer went on to explore a third island. There they were sighted by a party of natives who happened to be in the employ of an Australian Navy coastwatcher secretly based on Kolombangara. Once the existence and location of the PT 109 survivors was reported, rescue followed swiftly.

When stateside newspapers learned of the story they began referring to Jack as a war hero, but Jack, though now eligible for leave, had no intention of resting on his laurels: he stayed on in the Solomons and, as commander of PT 59, took part in one more PT action off Bougainville in November. But thereafter his back began troubling him so much that he was ordered to return to the U.S. in late December. He was stationed in Miami, Florida, until late May 1944, when he returned to Boston for major disc surgery. Before entering the hospital he learned that he had been awarded the Navy and Marine Corps Medal for heroic conduct. It was while he was beginning his recuperation from the operation that he learned that on August 12 Joe, Jr., had been shot down and killed while piloting an RAF Liberator over the English Channel.

Previous pages: The October 1942 graduating class at the Melville, R.I., Motor Torpedo Boat Training Center. Jack is in the back row, seventh from the right.

Above: Joe Kennedy, Jr., in his Navy flying kit. He was killed in action in 1944.

Left: In early 1944 Jack, just back from the Solomons and awaiting back surgery, poses with LeMoyne Billings, one of his closest friends since their days together at the Choate School.

Right: In June 1944, fresh from surgery, Lieutenant John F. Kennedy receives the Navy and Marine Corps Medal.

NATIONAL
***
VETERANS HOUSING
CONFERENCE

'S NO
KE HO

CANDIDATE KENNEDY

LACE
ME
ONE

The death of Joe, Jr., was a grievous emotional blow to every member of the tight-knit Kennedy clan, but for Joe, Sr., it brought at added dimension of disappointment. Throughout the 1930s Old Joe's appetite for political power had been growing. With his vast wealth he could exercise great influence behind the scenes, but supreme political power, the kind available in America only via elective office, was beyond his grasp. It was not, however, necessarily beyond his son's grasp, and for years Joe, Sr., had consciously been grooming Joe, Jr., for a high political destiny. Now all these hopes and plans were in ruins.

But Joseph Patrick Kennedy was not a man easily thwarted. If it could not be Joe, Jr., then it must be Jack. Even before the war ended (in September 1945) and while Jack was still slowly recovering from his back surgery, Joe, Sr., was putting together the formidable machine that was to propel his second son into politics. Jack had not fully regained the use of his legs until early 1945, and he had received his medical discharge from the Navy in March. During the long convalescence that followed he did some travelling, dabbled in journalism, and listened to his father's rapidly maturing plans.

The senior Kennedy's initial target was a potentially vacant Congressional seat in Massachusetts's Eleventh Congressional District, a Boston Democratic strong-hold. Jack was of course not a Boston (or even a Massachusetts) resident, but that winter he moved to Boston, established a voting residence at 122 Bowdoin Street, and settled down to work with his political organization. The nucleus of that organization consisted of old political pros selected by his father – men such as Joseph L. Kane, a cousin of Joe's, whose motto was reputed to have been that politics, like war, requires only three things: money, money, and more money. But Jack soon enlarged this core group by bringing in a number of younger men, mostly war veterans, whom he took to calling his "Little Brain Trust". Whatever these recruits might have lacked in experience, there was no denying their energy and talent, and one of them, David F. Porter, would eventually come to be recognized as one of the shrewdest political strategist in the country.

Jack was still not an avowed candidate for any particular public office, but his organization certainly behaved as if he were. The immediate objective was to make his name familiar to the voting public. An advertising agency was retained, and it bombarded Boston readers with endless stories about PT 109, about the death of Joe, Jr., about the commissioning (in the Navy yard in the Eleventh Congressional District) of a new destroyer named *Joseph P. Kennedy, Jr.*, and so on. Jack,

Previous pages: As a first-term Congressman, Kennedy speaks to a veterans' group about the housing problem in 1948.

Left: Jean, Joe, Sr., and Rose at the launching of the destroyer *Joseph P. Kennedy, Jr.* It was commissioned in a navy yard in the district where Jack planned to run for Congress in 1946.

Right: Jack entered politics with formidable political backing – not least from his own family. He is seen here with grandfather "Honey Fitz" (l.) and Joe, Sr., two of the Democratic Party's great movers and shakers.

Left: Jack at a Memorial Day observance during his 1946 Congressional campaign.

Below: Not a natural orator, Jack steadily improved his public speaking technique in the 1946 campaign.

Bottom: Jack speaking with Boston's Archbishop Richard J. Cushing, a Kennedy family friend, in 1946.

meantime, was seizing every available opportunity to speak in public, from American Legion Posts and Rotary Clubs to meetings of the Gold Star Mothers of America. He was far from a natural orator, but he was nothing if not determined, and his speaking technique steadily improved.

In November 1945 the incumbent for the Eleventh Congressional District, Michael J. Curley, was elected mayor of Boston, thus (as the Kennedy's had anticipated) vacating his Congressional seat. Jack shrewdly refrained from announcing his candidacy for the seat until his name was well enough established in the minds of Boston voters so that the move would seem neither eccentric nor presumptuous. When he did finally announce, in mid-April 1946, the all-important Democratic primary was only two months away. The Kennedy 60-day electoral blitz that followed was a triumph of organization, brains, energy, and spending on a massive scale. By primary day on June 18 the exhausted Jack was close to physical collapse, but the campaign had succeeded brilliantly: Jack emerged with nearly twice as many votes as his closest rival. And that, in effect, meant that he had already won his Congressional seat, for in those days no Republican could hope to win a November election in the rock-solid Eleventh Congressional District.

If Massachusetts's Eleventh District was a Democratic bastion, the Eightieth U.S. Congress was anything but. Even though a Democrat, Harry S Truman, still occupied the White House, both houses of Congress were now firmly under Republican control, the Republican preponderance in the House of Representatives being a whopping 245 to 188. The House in 1947-1948 was therefore not a very promising arena for a

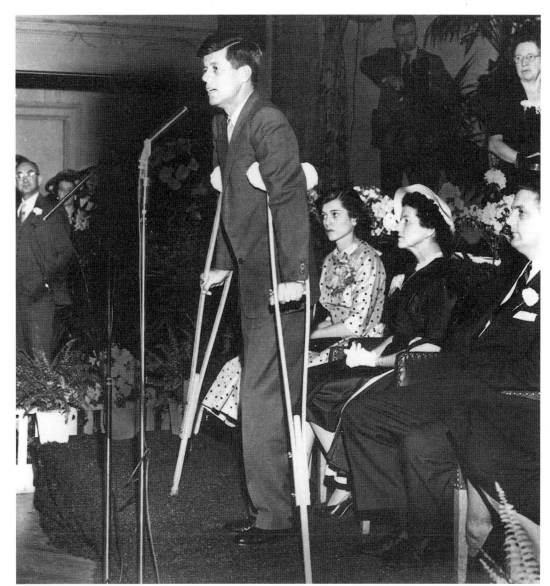

Previous pages: Jack on the hustings in 1946. The 60-day electoral blitz that won him his Congressional seat was a triumph of political skill and lavish spending.

Left: Congressman Kennedy on an inspection of the Boston waterfront. Jack always kept his fences mended back home.

Left below: Jack flanked by two of his best campaigners: his grandmother and "Honey Fitz" Fitzgerald.

Right: During Jack's run for the Senate in 1952 his back problem sometimes required him to campaign on crutches.

Right below: Jack and Henry Cabot Lodge, the Republican Senator who lost his seat to Jack in the 1952 campaign.

minority-party freshman who wanted to associate his name with important legislation, a fact that may in part account for Jack's generally lackluster (though certainly not discreditable) performance during his first term. He was unsuccessful both in supporting the Taft-Ellender-Wagner Housing Bill (for federally-financed slum clearance and new construction) and in opposing the Taft-Hartley Labor Act (which curtailed the power of labor unions), and the rest of his voting record similarly deviated little from the Democratic mainstream. Meantime, he was extremely careful about keeping his fences well mended back home in the Eleventh District.

During the late summer of 1947, while Jack was on a between-Congressional-sessions trip to England, he again fell victim to disease. The Kennedy organization blandly described his illness as a flare-up of malaria, but apparently it was far more serious than that. Though confirmation is lacking, it probably was Addison's Disease, a treatable but essentially incurable malfunction of the adrenal glands. There were reports that at one point his condition was so grave that he was given the last sacraments, but neither then nor later was the Kennedy family ever willing to provide a full explanation of this mysterious episode.

Jack was twice re-elected to Congress, but though the Democrats were back in control of the House during his last two terms, he still failed to make much of an im-

pression as a Representative. It may be, however, that by this time his ambitions were already turning to higher things. In any event, in April 1952 he announced that that November he would be a candidate for the Massachusetts Senate seat then held by Republican Henry Cabot Lodge, Jr. The decision was not without its risks. The popular Lodge, a scion of one of Boston's oldest and most distinguished families, would be no pushover, especially if the Republican standard-bearer

Left: Jack at the Democratic National Convention in 1952. He would offer himself as a nominee in 1956.

Left below: On September 12, 1953, 10 months after he had won his Senate seat, Jack married Jacqueline Bouvier in a glittering ceremony in Newport, Rhode Island.

Right: Jack with Gov. Adlai Stevenson in 1952. He would fail in his bid to become Stevenson's presidential running-mate in 1956.

Below: Jack and Jacqueline (Jackie) at their wedding. The gracious and beautiful Jackie would prove a great asset to Jack's career.

that November were to be the probably-unbeatable Dwight D. Eisenhower. (Ike would in fact become the Republican presidential nominee in July.) Yet the Kennedys now had almost unlimited faith in the power of their Massachusetts political machine, and they were convinced that they could prevail.

During the hard-fought campaign Jack found time to begin a serious pursuit of Jacqueline Lee Bouvier, the glamorous daughter of financier John V. Bouvier, 3rd, and, since 1940, step-daughter of Washington and Newport investment banker Hugh D. Auchincloss. Debutante of the year in 1947, she had studied at Vassar and the Sorbonne and had been graduated from George Washington University in 1951. Thanks to the rigors of campaigning, Jack's courtship at first was, as Jacqueline later said, "spasmodic," but after Jack upset Lodge in November by a big 71,000-vote margin, the affair became more intense, and the next year, on September 12, 1953, the couple was married by Archbishop Richard Cushing in a glittering ceremony in Newport.

Jack's first two years in the Senate were relatively colorless: he devoted much time to matters of local interest to Massachusetts voters and seemed loath to take clearcut stands on controversial issues – including the fulminating issue of McCarthyism. During the autumn of 1954 his back pain became so nearly intolerable that in October he entered a New York hospital for a highly dangerous (because of his apparently chronic adrenal malfunction) double fusion operation. Though Jack narrowly survived it, the surgery itself was reasonably successful,but not until May 1955 would he be well enough to return – on crutches – to the Senate.

During his long convalescence Jack, with the help of Theodore C. Sorensen, a friend from Jack's Harvard days, wrote another book. This was *Profiles in Courage,*

stories of eight Senators who had "put their nation and their conscience ahead of their political careers." When published, the book would sell extremely well and would eventually be awarded a Pulitzer Prize. But it would also give rise to a famous jibe leveled at Jack by those who felt his stand on the outrageous red-baiting of Joseph McCarthy had been too weak-kneed: "Please, Senator, a little less profile and a little more courage."

By the time Jack returned to Capitol Hill in May 1955 the Senate had already censured Senator McCarthy,

and that particular issue was fading away. But Jack did now seem to be showing an increased interest in other national and international matters, and, as his voting record became more decisive, his standing among his colleagues improved, though perhaps not quite enough for what the Kennedy team had in mind next. In 1956 they began lobbying hard to persuade the Democratic presidential nominee, Adlai E. Stevenson, to name Jack as his running mate, but in the end Stevenson left the choice open to the convention delegates, and Estes Kefauver was chosen instead. It was probably just as well for Jack, since in the election that fall the Eisenhower-Nixon ticket beat the Democrats by a margin of 457 electoral votes to 73.

After 1956 it was clear to most people that Jack Kennedy now had his sights set on the presidency, though whether Joe, Sr., or the Kennedy political organization, or Jack himself, had ever really had any other goal in mind during the decade past may be doubted. First he had to be re-elected to the Senate, but for the potent Kennedy political machine that was no great problem: Jack won his re-election in 1958 by a margin of nearly 875,000 votes. Thereafter Jack's Senate voting record on a range of highly visible issues, from public welfare to civil liberties, began to assume a consistently liberal aspect. In a political sense, he was rapidly establishing both his position and his persona. At the same time, the frequency of his public speaking markedly increased, as did the volume of personal publicity about him: pic-

Left above: After his back surgery in the fall of 1954 Jack was able to return to his Senate office only in May of 1955.

Left: While recovering from his back surgery Jack, with the help of an old Harvard friend, Ted Sorensen (l.), wrote *Profiles in Courage.*

Above: Jack autographing his book, *Profiles in Courage.*

Right: Jack getting ready to introduce a 1955 TV program based on *Profiles in Courage.*

1956
DEMOCRATIC
NATIONAL
CONVENTION

OUR CHOICE

tures and stories about him and Jacqueline (now called by everyone "Jackie") began to deluge the media. When, on January 2, 1960, he formally declared his candidacy for the presidency, there can have been few Americans left who were taken wholly by surprise.

Jack Kennedy's march towards the presidency during the next ten months has since been called a textbook example of political professionalism in action. He campaigned doggedly in state primary after state primary, and even in those states where voters hardly knew him his relentlessly efficient political organization never let him down when winning was crucial. He entered the Democratic National Convention in July the evident frontrunner, won the nomination on the first ballot, and then astutely picked the most dangerous of his former rivals, Texas Senator Lyndon B. Johnson, as his running mate.

So far, so good; but now the real battle began. Jack's tough, hard-fighting Republican opponent, Vice President Richard M. Nixon, was only four years older than Jack, but he was more politically prominent and came from a much more important state (California) – assets that went a long way toward countering Jack's vast financial resources and matchless political organization. In the end, the scales may have been tipped by a new, still only partially understood factor in American politics: television. In four nationally televised Kennedy-Nixon debates – the first such in U.S. history – Jack clearly emerged as the more personable of the two candidates. And TV helped in another way as well, for Jack and, especially, Jackie were as photogenic a couple as had ever appeared on the small screen. Yet down to the wire it was a close race, and when the November 8 votes were counted it was found that Jack had beaten Nixon by only two-tenths of one percent of the popular vote. It was the narrowest presidential mandate ever recorded in American history, but it was a mandate nonetheless. The years of relentless campaigning had achieved their goal. John Fitzgerald Kennedy was now the 35th president of the United States.

Previous pages: Jack at the 1956 Democratic National Convention.

Top: Jack and his opponent in the 1960 presidential election, Richard Nixon.

Above: Jackie campaigning for Jack in 1960.

Left: Senator Kennedy with a South African delegation.

Right above: Jack announcing his candidacy in 1960.

Right: Jack campaigning in Texas in 1960.

THE NEW FRONTIER

On Inauguration Day, January 20, 1961, Jack Kennedy made the single most famous speech in his life. Well-delivered and eloquent, his inaugural address built steadily to its memorable peroration: "And so my fellow Americans, ask not what your country can do for you – ask what you can do for your country." Never mind that the phrase had been borrowed (though virtually no one at the time realized it) from one of America's least memorable presidents, Warren G. Harding, as Jack delivered them, the words sounded like a clarion call to action and the dawning of a new spirit in national life.

Perhaps a more down-to-earth indication of what the new administration would be like came when Jack announced his cabinet appointments. Two Republicans were given key posts: business executive Robert S. McNamara went to Defense, and investment banker C. Douglas Dillon went to Treasury. Dean Rusk, the scholarly head of the Rockefeller Foundation, became the new secretary of state, and Stewart Udall, a conservation-minded Democratic Congressman from Arizona, became secretary of the interior. Only one appointment – that of attorney general – was truly controversial: it went to Jack's younger brother, Robert.

Questions of nepotism aside, "Bobby" Kennedy had other political liabilities. He was only 35 but was already detested by most of organized labor for his earlier part in investigations of labor racketeering. He would, as well, soon win the enmity of FBI Director J. Edgar Hoover, one of the great hidden (and not altogether benign) powers in Washington politics. But he was also extremely intelligent, tough, full of political savvy, and as fiercely loyal to Jack as only another Kennedy clan member could be. Jack was by now so dependent on his aid and counsel that the new president was prepared to face whatever adverse comment Bobby's appointment might provoke.

Jack – or JFK, as he now preferred to be called – had named his program for America "The New Frontier,"

and one of its first initiatives came in March with the creation of the Peace Corps, an organization of volunteer specialists who were to assist underdeveloped countries with on-the-scene labor and advice. Appointed to head the operation was Sargent Shriver, husband of JFK's sister Eunice. Although critics at first scoffed at what they considered the naive idealism of the project, the Peace Corps would ultimately prove to be one of the administration's more solid successes. But before that could happen, or before any more aspects of The New Frontier could be revealed, the Kennedy administration was to suffer what amounted to a major foreign policy disaster.

Late in the second Eisenhower administration the U.S. government had allowed itself to be drawn into a highly dubious scheme (mainly promoted by the CIA

Previous pages: Jack with brother Bobby in 1957. Bobby would be President Kennedy's attorney general.

Left above: JFK confers with his presidential predecessor, Dwight D. Eisenhower.

Left below: JFK announces his Peace Corps program at the University of Michigan in early 1961.

Right: The swearing-in of the Kennedy cabinet in 1961.

Below: JFK delivering his historic inaugural address.

Left: The Kennedys greet the noted cellist Pablo Casals at a White House reception.

Below: Astronaut John Glenn describes his space flight to JFK in 1962.

Bottom: JFK's first meeting with Soviet Premier Nikita Khrushchev, in Vienna, 1961.

Right: JFK and Jackie pose for a formal portrait in the redecorated Oval Room of the White House.

but also endorsed by the Pentagon) whereby the U.S. would lend covert material support to anti-communist Cuban exiles who meant to invade Cuba and overthrow the Marxist regime of Fidel Castro. JFK was of course informed of the plan (then well advanced) when he took office, but though uneasy, he did not cancel it. As a result, on April 17 about 1400 invaders appeared in Cuba's Bahia de Cochinos (Bay of Pigs), waded on shore, and in the next three days were virtually all killed or captured by vastly more numerous and better-equipped Cuban army regulars.

The political backlash from this humiliating fiasco was severe. It was impossible for the U.S. government to deny involvement, and while American hawks and doves might disagree about what should or shouldn't have been done, no one had a good word to say about what *had* been done. JFK grimly took responsibility for the debacle, but his relations with at least some of his military and civilian advisers were never quite the same thereafter.

Yet it was astonishing how quickly he recovered from this setback. By early May, buoyed by the success of NASA's *Freedom 7* mission, which put an American, Alan B. Shepard, Jr., briefly into space for the first time, JFK felt confident enough to begin preparing a proposal to Congress for a $9-billion space program that was intended to put an American on the moon by 1971. Then, later in the month, he embarked on a series of trips abroad which soon developed into a kind of public relations triumph, thanks perhaps especially to Jackie, whose beauty, poise, and style thawed the hearts of even the crustiest European leaders (France's imperious Charles de Gaulle, among them) and made her the overnight toast of the continent.

Indeed, it is difficult to overestimate the role that Jackie Kennedy would play in establishing the "Camelot" legend that we now associate with the Kennedy years. Her tasteful restoration of the White House, her elegant official entertainments (graced by such cultural

luminaries as world-famous cellist Pablo Casals), and, above all, her compelling personal charm and dignity made her seem a fairytale princess come to life. She set international styles not only in dress and coiffure but even in manners and bearing, and neither the public nor the media ever seemed able to get enough of her. She embellished JFK's presidency to an astonishing degree, and when, years later, it was revealed that JFK had been extravagantly unfaithful to her, not even his most ardent admirers could wholly forgive him.

For the remainder of 1961 the White House remained largely preoccupied with foreign affairs. The USSR's aggressive and bumptious premier, Nikita Khrushchev, having wrongly equated JFK's youth with weakness, kept up steady pressure on the new president by encouraging communist insurgency in Southeast Asia, ignoring nuclear test ban negotiations, demanding recognition of East German sovereignty, and crudely attempting to force the Western powers out of Berlin. The tense Berlin situation came to a head in August when the Soviets sealed off East Berlin behind the infamous Berlin Wall. JFK responded by calling up U.S. reserves and sending an armored convoy into West Berlin, after which the crisis lapsed into a kind of sullen stalemate. But communist prodding in Asia did prompt JFK to increase military aid to South Vietnam, thus contributing to the accelerating slide (begun under Eisenhower) that would eventually embroil America in the unhappiest of its wars. Perhaps the brightest achievement of JFK's foreign policy that year came with the enactment of the Alliance for Progress, a program providing long-term U.S. loans for housing, health, and education in Latin America that would do much to improve intra-hemisphere relations.

Although JFK's own family was burgeoning (daughter Caroline had been born on November 27, 1957, and John, Jr., on November 25, 1960), tragedy struck the Kennedy clan itself when its patriarch, Joe, Sr., suffered a stroke in December. He would never

Left above: JFK discussing the worsening situation in Southeast Asia at a March 1961 press conference.

Left: Promoting the Alliance for Progress, JFK speaks to an audience in Costa Rica.

Above: JFK and Jackie with their children – John Jr., and Caroline – in 1962.

Right: Caroline Kennedy and her pony, Macaroni, on the White House's South Lawn.

fully recover from it, but he would live long enough (until 1969) to learn of his son's assassination and the end of another of his dreams.

For much of 1962 JFK attempted to concentrate on domestic issues, but with mixed success. Though he had Democratic majorities in both the Senate and House, the overall mood of Congress was conservative, and many New Frontier initiatives suffered accordingly. JFK managed to get through a Trade Expansion Act (that enabled him to reduce tariffs in order to promote foreign trade) and a Drug Industry Act (that increased federal powers to regulate the introduction of new pharmaceuticals into the market). But Congress thwarted his efforts to create an Urban Affairs Department, to control farm surpluses, to overhaul the national transportation system, and much else.

Apparently because of Congress's balkiness, JFK procrastinated on making good his campaign promises to reform civil rights legislation: it was not until November that he finally signed a comparatively minor order to prohibit discrimination in federally-assisted housing. But on at least one highly visible civil rights issue his hand was forced. In defiance of a federal court order, Mississippi had refused to permit a black man, James H. Meredith, to register in the state university. JFK could not let this direct constitutional challenge go unanswered, and on September 10, surrounded by a phalanx of U.S. marshals and other federal lawmen, Meredith entered the university and was enrolled. That night the town of Oxford, site of the University of Mississippi, erupted in a riot that resulted in the death of two people and the injury of 375 others. To restore order, JFK had to send in the Army and federalize the Mississippi National Guard. For the remainder of Meredith's stay at the Unversity of Mississippi he was kept constantly under federal protection.

JFK had similarly given a tough response to a direct challenge earlier in the year when, having interpreted a price-rise by a group of steel companies as a violation of earlier understandings, he threatened the companies

Left: The Kennedy clan in Hyannis Port in 1962, at the birthday party for Joe, Sr.

Above: JFK with the National Council on Senior Citizens.

Above right: JFK speaks at an ILGWU housing project.

Right: JFK delivers his 1962 State of Union Address. Behind him: Vice President Lyndon Johnson and Speaker of the House John McCormack.

29 OCTOBER 1962

MRBM LAUNCH SITE 3
SAN CRISTOBAL, CUBA

ERECTOR REMOVED
FROM LAUNCH POSITIONS

LAUNCH STAND REMAINING

LAUNCH STAND REMAINING

ERECTOR REMOVED
FROM LAUNCH POSITION

CAMOUFLAGED
MISSILE TRANSPORTER
REMOVED

CONTINUED CONSTRUCTION

LAUNCH STAND
REMAINING

ERECTOR REMOVED
FROM LAUNCH POSITION

with such severe retaliation that they were forced to back down. It was perhaps because Nikita Khrushchev still failed to grasp this deep-seated combative streak in JFK that in the fall of 1962 the Soviet premier blundered into precipitating what would prove to be the gravest crisis of the entire Cold War.

Late in August U.S. reconnaissance planes had taken photographs of launching sites for Soviet-made ground-to-air missiles under construction in Cuba. JFK

reported this to the American people on September 4, saying that the U.S. was prepared to use "whatever means that may be necessary" to prevent Cuba from "taking action against any part of the Western hemisphere". The Soviets dismissed this warning, saying that the missiles were solely defensive and that the U.S. was merely using them as an excuse for a planned aggression against Cuba. The situation worsened steadily and then, in mid-October, escalated to all-out crisis when reconnaissance photos revealed than an intermediate-range ballistic missile site was also being built in Cuba. In a televised address on October 22 the president accused the Soviets of making "false statements about their intentions," indicated that any Cuban attack on the U.S. would be regarded as originating in Moscow, and announced the beginning of a total U.S. air and naval blockade of Cuba – itself legally an act of war.

For four nerve-wracking days it seemed that the world was teetering on the brink of nuclear holocaust. Then, on the 26th, JFK received a rambling cable from Khrushchev that suggested to White House analysts that Soviet resolve might be crumbling. And so it was: by the 28th the Soviets had agreed to dismantle the Cuban sites in return for a face-saving U.S. commitment to dismantle some of its own sites in Turkey. The world could breathe normally again, and John F. Kennedy had fought and won the most dangerous contest of his life.

Left above: A picture taken by a US reconnaissance plane of the intermediate-range ballistic missile site being built at San Cristobal, Cuba, in October 1962.

Left: A Soviet cargo ship laden with missiles en route to Cuba in 1962.

Above: JFK announces to the nation that the US intends to mount a total air-and-sea blockade of the island of Cuba (October 22, 1962).

Right: JFK meets with Soviet diplomats during the Missile Crisis. Foreign Minister Andrei Gromyko is seated on the president's right.

CAMELOT'S END

Although in the eyes of the world JFK had emerged from the Cuban Missile Crisis with vastly increased stature, Congress still seemed detemined to play politics-as-usual, and as 1963 dawned it looked as though the president's New Frontier initiatives might fare no better than they had in 1962. But 1963 was not destined to be a year of routine legislative in-fighting. Instead, it was a year in which the nation and its government were obliged to confront the festering civil rights issue as never before.

Early in April blacks in Birmingham, Alabama, led by the charismatic Rev. Martin Luther King, Jr., began a series of peaceful anti-discrimination protests. The demonstrations grew in size and publicity as the local protestors were joined by hundreds of out-of-state Freedom Marchers, many of them young students. On May 2 Birmingham authorities arrested some 500 demonstrators, and others were violently attacked by mobs the next day. JFK at first took the position that the federal government could not legally intervene, but as the violence worsened he was compelled to act and in the end had to send in federal troops to restore order.

Similar racial confrontations then erupted in other cities. Again JFK tried initially to deal with them by con-ciliation, but the pressures for federal intervention grew inexorably. In June, for example, in a replay of the University of Mississippi situation, Governor George Wallace tried to prevent two black students from registering at the University of Alabama, and again JFK had to federalize the state National Guard in order to make Wallace relent. Before the month was out, the president had bowed to the inevitable and had sub-mitted to Congress a Civil Rights Act aimed at ending discrimination in many sectors of American society. Though JFK would not live to see it enacted, it would form the basis of the great Civil Rights Act of 1964. Meantime, to impress upon Congress and the nation

the gravity of the problem, on August 28 200,000 civil rights demonstrators marched peacefully into Washington, D.C., to, among other things, hear Martin Luther King deliver the most famous and moving speech of his life: "I Have a Dream".

Two months earlier JFK had made a famous speech of his own. On June 26, standing before some one million cheering West Berliners, he had reaffirmed the U.S. commitment to West Berlin's security in the ringing phrase, "Ich bin ein Berliner". By that time he was

Previous pages: During the civil rights demonstrations that occurred in Birmingham, Alabama, in 1963 a police dog attacks a marcher.

Above: RFK and his attorney general and closest adviser, Robert F. "Bobby" Kennedy.

Left: Bobby Kennedy meets with civil rights leaders in 1963. On his right: Martin Luther King, Jr. To his left: Roy Wilkins, Lyndon Johnson, and Walter Reuther.

Right above: JFK delivering his "Ich bin ein Berliner" speech in June 1963.

Right: During his 1963 trip to Berlin, JFK visited the infamous Berlin Wall.

already aware that the Soviets might at last be willing to sign a limited nuclear test ban treaty, and this small but highly significant step towards reducing Cold War tensions was in fact taken on August 5.

In that same eventful summer Jacqueline Kennedy gave birth to, but within 39 hours lost, a baby boy, Patrick Bouvier Kennedy. She was, however, sufficiently recovered by November to accompany her husband on a three-day tour of Texas, where she was soon to take part in an even more devastating tragedy.

At midday on November 22 the Kennedys were riding in the back of an open limousine leading a four-car motorcade that was slowly making its way through the crowded streets of Dallas. Sitting on jump seats ahead of the Kennedys were Texas Governor John B. Connally and his wife. At 12:30 PM, as the motorcade passed the Texas School Book Depository Building, shots rang out in quick succession. One bullet struck the president in the shoulder, another in the back of the head. A third bullet seriously, though not fatally, wounded Governor Connally. By the time the speeding limousine reached Parkland Hospital (in about five minutes) John F. Kennedy was, for all medical purposes, already dead.

Though some conspiracy theorists have always denied it, overwhelming evidence suggests that a dis-

Left: JFK and Jackie descend from their plane in Dallas, Texas, on November 22, 1963, to begin their fateful last day together.

Above: This photograph of JFK, Jackie, and Governor and Mrs. John Connally of Texas was taken roughly 60 seconds before the fusillade that wounded the governor and killed the president.

Above right: Jackie leans over the fatally wounded JFK as a Secret Service agent scrambles onto the car.

Right: The probable murderer of the president, disturbed loner Lee Harvey Oswald.

Left: The president's casket is brought to the White House on November 23.

Below: Jackie, flanked by Robert and Edward Kennedy, walks in the solemn funeral procession down Pennsylvania Avenue on the 25th.

Right: The president's flag-draped casket, carried on a caisson, in the procession down Pennsylvania Avenue.

Right bottom: JFK spends a quiet moment with his son, John, Jr., less than ten weeks before the fatal trip to Dallas in November.

turbed loner named Lee Harvey Oswald was the sole assassin. But the fact that before he could be brought to trial Oswald was himself murdered by another strange character, Dallas nightclub-owner Jack Ruby, certainly did nothing to quiet the theorists.

The shocked dismay with which the world greeted the news of John Kennedy's murder has had few parallels in this century. For days millions of people both here and abroad sat by television sets as if transfixed, watching the mournful unfolding of the president's funerary rites – the lying in state of the flag-draped coffin in the Capitol rotunda, with a veiled Jackie Kennedy and her two children standing watch; the slow funeral procession down Pennsylvania Avenue on the 25th, with eight heads of state and 10 prime ministers among the host of mourners; the solemn burial at Arlington National Cemetery while 50 USAF jets roared overhead; a band in West Berlin playing *Ich Hatt' einenKameraden*, dirge of the fallen soldier; and many other images that people who lived through the time still find painful to remember.

Was this vast outpouring of grief excessive? John Kennedy's term of office had, after all, been short – only about a thousand days – and though it had been dramatic, it had been no more than moderately successful in terms of legislation enacted. Indeed, even at the time, some critics were calling it a triumph of style over substance. But perhaps to dwell overmuch on John Kennedy's record is to miss the point. People did not grieve solely for the man and his stricken family, or for the end of some semi-mythical White House "Camelot". They grieved as well for all the unfulfilled hopes and aspirations that John Kennedy had somehow come to represent. As James Reston, dean of Washington correspondents, put it: "What was killed was not only the president but the promise." In a world desperate for promise – then, as it is today – that was probably no small thing to mourn.

INDEX

Page numbers in *italics* indicate illustrations

Picture Credits

All photographs courtesy of
the John F. Kennedy Library,
Boston, Massachusetts, except
the following:

**Bachrach/John F. Kennedy
Library:** 15(top).
Black Star: Charles Moore:
56-57; **Flip Schulke:**
43(bottom); **Werner Wolf:**
48(bottom).
**College of the Holy Cross/John
F. Kennedy Library:** 8(bottom).
U.S. Army Photograph: 31(top
left), 54(both).
**U.S. Naval Photographic
Center:** 20(top).